Prologue

"In the midst of movement and chaos, keep stillness inside of you." — *Deepak Chopra*

The clamor of city life was a constant backdrop to my early career—a symphony of honking horns, ringing phones, and the relentless tapping of keyboards. As a young professional eager to make my mark, I embraced the hustle with open arms. Success, I believed, was a destination marked by promotions, accolades, and a schedule so packed that sleep became a luxury.

One evening, after yet another twelve-hour workday, I found myself alone in my office, the glow of the computer screen casting long shadows in the empty room. Exhaustion weighed heavily on me, yet my mind refused to rest. A question lingered: *Is this what success truly feels like?*

That moment of introspection set me on a path of exploration and discovery. Determined to find answers, I took a leap of faith and embarked on a journey that would span continents and cultures.

In Vietnam, I met a fisherman named Tran, whose simple life by the Mekong Delta radiated a contentment I hadn't felt in years. His days were a harmonious blend of work, family, and leisure—an embodiment of balance without the trappings of modern success.

In India, I sat with monks in the Himalayas, learning the art of mindfulness and the profound impact of living in the present moment. Their serenity was a stark contrast to the constant unrest I felt despite my achievements.

Australia's vast landscapes taught me the significance of grounding oneself, while the shamans in Thailand introduced me to the healing power of nature and spiritual connection. In the bustling streets of Tokyo, professionals practiced Ikigai—a reason for being—balancing their passions with their professions.

Each encounter peeled back layers of my preconceived notions about success. I realized that while I had been climbing the corporate ladder, I had lost touch with the very essence of what it meant to live a fulfilled life.

This book is the culmination of that transformative journey. It weaves together the wisdom of the many individuals I met—from monks and shamans to fishermen and business professionals—and the lessons they imparted about achieving true balance.

My hope is that through these pages, you'll find guidance, inspiration, and practical tools to navigate your own path toward a harmonious life. This isn't a prescription but an invitation to explore, reflect, and define balance on your own terms.

As you embark on this journey, remember that balance is not a finite goal but a continuous practice. It's about making mindful choices that align with your values and embracing the ebb and flow of life with grace.

Welcome to a voyage of self-discovery. May it lead you to a life rich in purpose, joy, and equilibrium.

Let the journey begin.

"It was 11:45 PM on a Thursday, and Alex found himself staring blankly at the glowing screen of his laptop. The emails kept coming, the projects kept piling up, and the deadline for his latest assignment loomed ominously over his head. In the other room, his friends were celebrating a milestone in their careers—laughing, unwinding, living. But Alex couldn't join them. He had traded in his nights, weekends, and even his hobbies for a job that demanded more than he ever imagined. On the surface, Alex seemed like a rising star in his company, yet deep inside, he was exhausted and disillusioned. Something was missing, but he didn't know what it was—or how to fix it."

Alex's story isn't unique—it's a reflection of the challenges that many young professionals face in today's fast-paced world. Alex had always been driven. Graduating at the top of his class and landing a coveted position at a well-known tech company was a dream come true. But what came next was something he wasn't prepared for.

At first, the long hours didn't bother him. He saw it as part of paying his dues, a necessary sacrifice to climb the career ladder. "I'll rest when I'm successful," he would tell himself. But as months turned into years, the lines between his work and personal life began to blur. Slowly, his social life took a back seat. His once-regular gym visits became rare, and phone calls to family were hurried or forgotten altogether. It wasn't that he didn't care —he simply didn't have the time.

Alex began to notice subtle changes. His energy levels plummeted, and he found himself constantly on edge. Even when he wasn't working, his mind was. The once joyful career that fueled his ambition had now become a source of stress and anxiety. Every time his phone buzzed with a work notification, his heart raced. It wasn't just his time that work had taken—it was his peace of mind.

The tipping point came one weekend when Alex was meant to be at a close friend's wedding. He had planned for months to take the weekend off, yet as the event approached, a high-stakes project suddenly landed on his desk. His manager assured him it was critical and couldn't wait. Torn between his professional duties and personal commitments, Alex chose to stay back and finish the project. It was a decision he would come to regret.

As he worked late that night, his phone pinged with photos from the wedding—a celebration he had missed for something he could barely remember two weeks later. That night, Alex realized something had to change. It wasn't just about missing one wedding; it was about the cumulative effect of missing life. His work was important, yes, but at what cost?

This moment of clarity was the catalyst for Alex's journey toward finding balance—a journey many of us are on. Like Alex, we often think balance is a luxury, something we'll achieve once we reach a certain point in our careers. But the truth is, work-life balance isn't a destination; it's a practice. It's about making conscious decisions to protect our time, our health, and our relationships while still striving for professional success.

the Book's Purpose

Work-life balance isn't just a nice-to-have; it's essential for long-term success and fulfillment. This book is your guide to navigating the pressures of modern professional life while still making space for what truly matters—your well-being, your passions, and your relationships. Just like Alex, you can find a way to thrive in both your work and personal life. Let's explore how to make that a reality.

Chapter 1: Understanding the Imbalance

"Balance is not something you find; it's something you create." —Jana Kingsford

In our fast-paced, always-connected world, the pursuit of professional success often overshadows the equally important need for personal fulfillment. As young professionals, we're inundated with messages glorifying the "grind" and the relentless hustle required to get ahead. But at what cost?

In this chapter, we'll explore how an excessive focus on work can lead to an imbalanced life. We'll identify the signs of this imbalance, delve into its psychological and physical impacts, and challenge the prevailing myths of hustle culture. By the end, you'll have a clearer understanding of where you stand and how redefining success can set the foundation for a more balanced and fulfilling life.

Identifying the Current State of Imbalance

1. The Modern Professional's Dilemma

The lines between work and personal life have become increasingly blurred. With smartphones and laptops, work follows us home, to the gym, even on vacation. The expectation to be always available can make it feel impossible to truly disconnect.

- **Constant Connectivity:** Emails, messages, and notifications demand immediate attention.
- **Blurring Boundaries:** Remote work and flexible hours can lead to longer workdays.
- **Cultural Pressures:** Societal norms often equate busyness with success.

2. Signs You're Focusing Too Much on Work

- **Neglecting Personal Relationships:** Missing family events or canceling plans with friends.
- **Physical Exhaustion:** Chronic fatigue despite adequate

sleep.
- **Mental Preoccupation:** Inability to stop thinking about work during personal time.
- **Loss of Interest in Hobbies:** Activities that once brought joy now feel like chores.

3. Self-Reflection Questions

- Do you feel guilty when you're not working?
- Have you sacrificed sleep or meals to get work done?
- Is your identity tied solely to your professional role?

The Psychological and Physical Toll of Imbalance

1. Psychological Impacts

- **Increased Stress and Anxiety:** Constant pressure can lead to heightened stress levels.
- **Burnout:** Emotional, physical, and mental exhaustion caused by prolonged stress.
- **Depression:** Feelings of sadness or emptiness resulting from chronic imbalance.

2. Physical Consequences

- **Health Issues:** Elevated risk of heart disease, hypertension, and weakened immune system.
- **Sleep Disturbances:** Insomnia or restless sleep due to overactive thoughts.
- **Poor Nutrition:** Skipping meals or relying on fast food because of time constraints.

3. Effects on Relationships

- **Emotional Detachment:** Difficulty connecting with loved ones.
- **Communication Breakdown:** Misunderstandings arising from lack of quality time.
- **Social Isolation:** Withdrawing from social activities and support networks.

Breaking the Myth of "Hustle Culture" and Redefining Success

1. The Allure of Hustle Culture

- **Social Media Influence:** Platforms showcasing entrepreneurs who work around the clock.
- **Fear of Falling Behind:** Worrying that taking a break means missing opportunities.
- **Validation Through Busyness:** Equating a packed schedule with importance and success.

2. The Downside of Perpetual Hustle

- **Diminished Productivity:** Overwork can lead to mistakes and decreased efficiency.
- **Creativity Drain:** Lack of rest stifles innovation and problem-solving abilities.
- **Life Imbalance:** Sacrificing personal growth and relationships for work.

3. Redefining Success

- **Holistic Achievement:** Success encompasses professional accomplishments and personal well-being.
- **Quality Over Quantity:** Focusing on impactful work rather than endless tasks.
- **Personal Fulfillment:** Pursuing passions and interests outside of work.

4. Embracing a New Mindset

- **Self-Compassion:** Allowing yourself grace to rest and recharge.
- **Mindful Living:** Being present in each moment, whether at work or in personal time.
- **Value-Driven Goals:** Aligning your actions with your core values.

Checklist: Assessing Your Work-Life Balance

Use the following checklist to evaluate your current state:

1. **Work Hours:**
   - Do you work more than 50 hours a week?
   - Do you take work home regularly?

2. **Personal Time:**
    - Do you have hobbies you engage in weekly?
    - Do you spend quality time with friends and family?

3. **Health:**
    - Are you experiencing frequent stress-related symptoms?
    - Do you exercise regularly and maintain a balanced diet?

4. **Mental State:**
    - Do you feel anxious or guilty when not working?
    - Are you satisfied with your life outside of work?

5. **Technology Use:**
    - Do you check emails or messages during personal time?
    - Is it hard for you to disconnect from work devices?

Scoring:

- **Mostly Yes:** You may be experiencing an imbalance that needs attention.
- **Mostly No:** You are likely maintaining a healthier work-life balance.

Exercise: Personal Balance Inventory

Objective: To identify areas of imbalance and understand their impact on your life.

Instructions:

1. **List Key Life Areas:** Examples include Career, Family, Friends, Health, Personal Growth, Leisure.

2. **Rate Each Area (1-10):**
    - **Time Investment:** How much time do you currently devote?
    - **Satisfaction Level:** How satisfied are you with this area?

3. **Identify Discrepancies:**
   - Where are you investing the most time?
   - Are high time investments leading to high satisfaction?

4. **Reflect:**
   - Write down any feelings or thoughts that arise during this exercise.
   - Note any surprises or areas that need attention.

Example:

Life Area	Time Investment (1-10)	Satisfaction Level (1-10)
Career	9	7
Family	3	5
Friends	2	4
Health	4	3
Personal Growth	5	6
Leisure	2	5

Reflection: The high time investment in career isn't equating to higher satisfaction in other areas. Health and leisure are notably low, indicating potential areas for rebalancing.

Action Plan: First Steps Toward Rebalance

1. **Set Clear Intentions**
   - **Define Priorities:** Choose one or two areas to focus on improving.
   - **Specific Goals:** Make your goals measurable (e.g., "Exercise three times a week").

2. **Establish Boundaries**
   - **Work Hours:** Set a time to stop working each day.
   - **Disconnect:** Turn off work notifications during personal time.

3. Schedule Personal Activities

- **Family and Friends:** Plan regular get-togethers or calls.
- **Hobbies:** Dedicate time each week to activities you enjoy.

4. Practice Mindfulness

- **Present Moment Awareness:** Engage fully in whatever you're doing without multitasking.
- **Stress Management Techniques:** Incorporate meditation, deep breathing, or yoga.

5. Seek Support

- **Accountability Partner:** Share your goals with someone who can encourage you.
- **Professional Help:** Consider coaching or counseling if needed.

Closing Thoughts

Recognizing and understanding the imbalance in your life is a courageous first step toward meaningful change. It's not about achieving a perfect balance but finding a rhythm that allows you to thrive both professionally and personally. Remember, redefining success on your terms is not only empowering but essential for a fulfilling life.

As you move forward, keep this in mind:

"You will never feel truly satisfied by work until you are satisfied by life." — Heather Schuck

Let's continue this journey together, exploring practical strategies and insights to help

you achieve the harmony you deserve.

Chapter 2: Defining Your Core Values

Next Steps:

- **Reflect on this chapter's content.**
- **Complete the exercises honestly.**
- **Begin implementing one action item this week.**

In the next chapter, we'll delve deeper into **Defining Your Core Values**, a crucial step in aligning your life with what truly matters to you.

"The decisions we make are a reflection of our values and beliefs, and they are always a choice." — Louise L. Hay

Imagine setting out on a journey without a destination or a map. You might wander aimlessly, unsure of where you're heading or why you're even on the road. Similarly, navigating life without a clear understanding of your core values can lead to feelings of confusion, dissatisfaction, and imbalance.

In this chapter, we'll embark on a journey of self-discovery to uncover what truly matters to you. By identifying and embracing your core values, you'll gain a compass to guide your decisions, align your actions with your beliefs, and ultimately create a more balanced and fulfilling life.

Discovering What Truly Matters in Life

1. Understanding Core Values

Core values are the fundamental beliefs that guide your behavior and decision-making. They are the principles that resonate deeply within you and define who you are at your core.

- **Personal Significance:** Values differ from person to person; what matters most to you might not be as important to someone else.
- **Foundation for Decisions:** They influence choices in your career, relationships, and personal growth.
- **Consistency:** Living in alignment with your values brings a sense of integrity and authenticity.

2. Common Core Values to Consider

- **Family:** Prioritizing relationships with family members.
- **Health:** Valuing physical and mental well-being.
- **Career Growth:** Aspiring for professional advancement and achievement.
- **Personal Growth:** Seeking continuous learning and self-improvement.
- **Freedom:** Desiring independence and the ability to make your own choices.
- **Integrity:** Upholding honesty and strong moral principles.
- **Creativity:** Valuing innovation and self-expression.
- **Compassion:** Caring deeply about others and acting with kindness.

3. Reflecting on Your Life

Consider moments when you felt truly fulfilled and content. What were you doing? Who were you with? These moments often align closely with your core values.

- **Peak Experiences:** Times when you felt happiest and most satisfied.
- **Times of Conflict:** Situations where you felt uneasy or conflicted may indicate when your values were compromised.

Aligning Work and Life with Personal Values

1. The Importance of Alignment

When your daily actions align with your core values, you experience harmony and satisfaction. Misalignment can lead to stress, frustration, and a sense of emptiness.

- **Consistency in Actions:** Ensures that your behavior reflects what you believe in.
- **Enhanced Well-being:** Alignment contributes to overall happiness and reduces internal conflict.
- **Authentic Relationships:** Enables deeper connections

with others who share or respect your values.

2. Assessing Alignment in Different Life Areas

- **Career:**
    - Does your job allow you to express your values?
    - Are you proud of the work you do and the company you work for?
- **Relationships:**
    - Do your relationships nurture and support your values?
    - Are you able to be yourself around friends and family?
- **Lifestyle Choices:**
    - How do your hobbies and interests reflect what you value?
    - Are your daily habits supporting your well-being?

3. Real-Life Example: Sophia's Journey

Sophia valued creativity and helping others. She worked in a high-paying corporate job but felt unfulfilled. After introspection, she realized her work didn't align with her values. She transitioned into a role at a non-profit organization where she could use her creativity to make a positive impact. This alignment brought her immense satisfaction and renewed energy.

How Core Values Influence Decision-Making and Priority Setting

1. A Guiding Framework

Core values act as a decision-making compass, helping you navigate choices big and small.

- **Clarity in Choices:** Simplifies decisions by filtering options through your values.
- **Priority Setting:** Helps you focus on what's truly important, making it easier to allocate time and resources.
- **Conflict Resolution:** Provides a basis for resolving

internal and external conflicts.

2. Decision-Making in Practice

- **Professional Decisions:**
    - Choosing a job offer that aligns with your value of work-life balance over one that demands excessive hours.
- **Personal Life Choices:**
    - Prioritizing time with loved ones if family is a top value, even if it means declining additional work assignments.
- **Financial Decisions:**
    - Investing in experiences like travel or education if personal growth and exploration are important to you.

3. Overcoming Challenges

Sometimes, you may face situations where values conflict or external pressures challenge your priorities.

- **Value Conflicts:** Recognize and address when two values compete (e.g., career advancement vs. family time).
- **External Expectations:** Stay true to your values despite societal pressures or expectations from others.

Checklist: Identifying Your Core Values

Use this checklist to begin identifying what you value most:

1. **Reflective Questions:**
    - What qualities do you admire in others?
    - When do you feel most authentic and true to yourself?
    - What motivates and energizes you?
2. **List of Common Core Values:**
    - **Achievement**
    - **Adventure**
    - **Balance**
    - **Community**

- **Compassion**
- **Creativity**
- **Family**
- **Friendship**
- **Health**
- **Integrity**
- **Learning**
- **Security**
- **Spirituality**
- **Wealth**

3. **Identifying Neglected Values:**
   - Are there values that are important to you but not currently reflected in your life?
   - What feelings arise when you consider these neglected areas?

Exercise: Value Mapping

Objective: To identify your top 5 core values and assess how well your current lifestyle aligns with them.

Instructions:

1. **Brainstorm Values:**
   - Write down all the values that resonate with you from the checklist above or any others that come to mind.

2. **Narrow Down Your Top 5:**
   - Reflect on each value's importance.
   - Choose the five that are most essential to your sense of self.

3. **Create a Value Map:**

Core Value	Current Alignment (1-10)	Notes
Example: Health	6	Exercise irregularly, need better diet

4. **Assess Alignment:**
   - Rate how well each value is reflected in your life (1 = not at all, 10 = fully aligned).
   - Add notes on why you gave each rating.
5. **Reflect:**
   - Where are the gaps?
   - How does misalignment affect your well-being?

Example Reflection:

- **Value:** Family
- **Alignment Rating:** 4
- **Notes:** Haven't been spending much time with family due to work commitments. Feel disconnected.

Action Plan: Creating a Values-Based Decision Framework

Objective: To use your core values as a guide when making decisions, ensuring alignment between your actions and what matters most to you.

Steps:

1. **Develop Your Framework:**
   - **Awareness:** Before making a decision, pause to consider your core values.
   - **Alignment Check:** Ask yourself, "Does this choice align with my values?"
   - **Long-Term Impact:** Consider how the decision will affect you in the long run, not just immediately.
2. **Implementing the Framework:**
   - **Scenario Planning:** Think through possible outcomes of each option in relation to your values.
   - **Prioritize Values:** In situations where values

conflict, decide which value takes precedence.
- **Seek Feedback:** Discuss significant decisions with trusted individuals who understand your values.

3. **Applying to Daily Decisions:**
- **Work Commitments:** Before taking on extra work, consider if it will impede on personal time and if it aligns with your value of balance.
- **Personal Life Choices:** Choose activities and relationships that support your values.
- **Time Management:** Allocate time based on your priorities, ensuring important values receive adequate attention.

Example Application:

- **Decision:** Offered a promotion that requires longer hours.
- **Values Involved:** Career Growth (important), Family Time (very important).
- **Framework Application:**
  - **Alignment Check:** Will the new role enhance my career but at the expense of family time?
  - **Long-Term Impact:** Could lead to career advancement but may strain family relationships.
  - **Decision:** Negotiate for flexible hours or support to maintain family time, or consider declining if alignment isn't possible.

Closing Thoughts

Uncovering and embracing your core values is a transformative step toward achieving work-life balance. By knowing what truly matters to you, decisions become clearer, priorities more defined, and life more fulfilling.

Remember, living in alignment with your values is an ongoing practice. It requires mindfulness, honesty, and sometimes, courage to make choices that honor who you are.

"Your values are your GPS. They guide you to your destination." — Dr. Steve Maraboli

Next Steps:

- **Complete the Value Mapping Exercise.**
- **Begin applying the Values-Based Decision Framework in daily life.**
- **Reflect on any changes in how you feel and interact with the world.**

In the next chapter, we'll explore **The Power of Time Management**, providing tools and techniques to help you make the most of your time and further support your journey toward balance.

Chapter 3: The Power of Time Management

"Time is the one thing we all have in common, but it's also the one thing that we all use differently." — Catherine Pulsifer

Time is our most valuable non-renewable resource. Yet, many of us find ourselves saying, "I wish there were more hours in a day." The truth is, it's not about having more time but making the most of the time we have. Effective time management is a cornerstone of achieving work-life balance. It allows us to fulfill our professional responsibilities while still making space for personal growth, relationships, and self-care.

In this chapter, we'll explore how mastering time management can transform your life. We'll introduce practical tools like the Eisenhower Matrix to help you prioritize tasks effectively. We'll also discuss strategies to break down overwhelming projects into manageable steps, empowering you to take control of your schedule and, ultimately, your life.

Mastering Time: The Key to Balance

1. The Importance of Time Management

- **Enhances Productivity:** Effective time management helps you focus on important tasks, reducing wasted time.
- **Reduces Stress:** Knowing what needs to be done and when alleviates anxiety and last-minute rushes.
- **Improves Quality of Life:** By allocating time wisely, you ensure that both work and personal life receive the attention they deserve.

2. Common Time Management Challenges

- **Procrastination:** Delaying tasks leads to increased stress and workload pile-up.
- **Distractions:** Social media, emails, and unplanned interruptions can derail your focus.

- **Overcommitting:** Taking on too many tasks makes it difficult to manage time effectively.

3. The Link Between Time Management and Balance

- **Work Creep:** Poor time management can cause work tasks to spill into personal time.
- **Neglected Priorities:** Without control over your time, important personal activities may be neglected.
- **Burnout Risk:** Constantly feeling overwhelmed can lead to physical and emotional exhaustion.

Introducing the Eisenhower Matrix

1. What Is the Eisenhower Matrix?

The Eisenhower Matrix, named after President Dwight D. Eisenhower, is a simple yet powerful tool for prioritizing tasks based on their urgency and importance.

- **Urgent Tasks:** Require immediate attention.
- **Important Tasks:** Contribute to long-term goals and values.

2. The Four Quadrants

- **Quadrant 1:** Urgent and Important (Do First)
- **Quadrant 2:** Important but Not Urgent (Schedule)
- **Quadrant 3:** Urgent but Not Important (Delegate)
- **Quadrant 4:** Neither Urgent nor Important (Eliminate)

3. How to Use the Matrix

- **List Your Tasks:** Write down all tasks you need to accomplish.
- **Assign to Quadrants:** Place each task into the appropriate quadrant.
- **Take Action:**
  - **Quadrant 1:** Handle these tasks immediately.
  - **Quadrant 2:** Schedule time to work on these tasks.
  - **Quadrant 3:** Delegate or reschedule if possible.
  - **Quadrant 4:** Eliminate these tasks to free up

time.

4. Benefits of the Eisenhower Matrix

- **Clarity:** Helps distinguish between what needs immediate attention and what can wait.
- **Efficiency:** Ensures you're working on tasks that align with your goals.
- **Balance:** Prevents less important tasks from consuming your time.

Breaking Down Overwhelming Tasks

1. The Problem with Big Tasks

Large projects can seem daunting, leading to procrastination and stress.

- **Psychological Barriers:** The sheer size can create fear of failure.
- **Lack of Direction:** Not knowing where to start hinders progress.

2. Strategies for Managing Big Tasks

- **Divide and Conquer:** Break the task into smaller, manageable steps.
- **Set Milestones:** Establish checkpoints to track progress.
- **Prioritize Subtasks:** Focus on one step at a time.

3. Tools to Assist

- **To-Do Lists:** Keep track of tasks and check them off as you complete them.
- **Project Management Apps:** Tools like Trello or Asana can help organize tasks visually.
- **SMART Goals:** Ensure each subtask is Specific, Measurable, Achievable, Relevant, and Time-bound.

4. The Benefits of Breaking Tasks Down

- **Reduces Overwhelm:** Smaller tasks feel more manageable.
- **Increases Motivation:** Completing subtasks provides a

sense of accomplishment.

- **Enhances Focus:** Allows you to concentrate on one aspect at a time.

Checklist: Assessing Your Time Management

Evaluate your current time management practices with the following questions:

1. **Planning and Prioritization**
   - Do you create daily or weekly schedules?
   - Do you prioritize tasks based on importance and urgency?
   - Are your goals clearly defined?

2. **Multitasking Habits**
   - Do you frequently switch between tasks?
   - Does multitasking improve or reduce your productivity?

3. **Meeting Deadlines**
   - Do you often miss personal or professional deadlines?
   - Are you realistic about the time needed for tasks?

4. **Distraction Management**
   - Are you easily distracted by emails, social media, or other interruptions?
   - Do you set aside specific times to check messages?

5. **Work-Life Boundaries**
   - Do work tasks encroach on your personal time?
   - Do you have difficulty saying no to additional work?

Reflection: Identify areas where your time management could improve. Recognizing these areas is the first step toward enhancing your work-life balance.

Exercise: Time Block Challenge

Objective: Allocate dedicated time blocks for various aspects of your life and assess the impact on your productivity and balance.

Instructions:

1. **Plan Your Week Ahead**
   - **Identify Core Activities:** List essential tasks for work, personal life, health, and leisure.
   - **Create a Schedule:** Use a planner or digital calendar to assign time blocks to each activity.

2. **Implement Time Blocks**
   - **Work Time:** Designate specific hours for work tasks.
   - **Family and Personal Time:** Schedule time for relationships and self-care.
   - **Health Activities:** Include exercise, meal preparation, and rest.
   - **Leisure:** Allocate time for hobbies and relaxation.

3. **Stick to Your Schedule**
   - **Commitment:** Treat each time block with equal importance.
   - **Minimize Distractions:** Turn off non-essential notifications during focused periods.

4. **End-of-Day Reflection**
   - **Assess Feelings:** Note your energy levels, stress, and satisfaction.
   - **Adjust as Needed:** Make changes to your schedule based on what works best.

5. **Weekly Review**
   - **Evaluate Impact:** Consider how the time blocking affected your balance.
   - **Plan for Next Week:** Adjust your time blocks to better suit your needs.

Example Time Block Schedule:

Time	Monday	Tuesday	Wednesday	Thursday	Friday
6 AM	Morning	Morning	Morning	Morning	Morning

- 7 AM	Workout	Workout	Workout	Workout	Workout
7 AM - 8 AM	Breakfast & Prep	Breakfast & Prep	Breakfast & Prep	Breakfast & Prep	Breakfast & Prep
8 AM - 12 PM	Work Projects	Work Projects	Work Projects	Work Projects	Work Projects
12 PM - 1 PM	Lunch Break	Lunch Break	Lunch Break	Lunch Break	Lunch Break
1 PM - 5 PM	Meetings & Emails	Client Work	Meetings & Emails	Client Work	Planning & Review
5 PM - 7 PM	Family Time	Personal Hobby	Family Time	Personal Hobby	Social Time
7 PM - 9 PM	Dinner & Relax	Dinner & Relax	Dinner & Relax	Dinner & Relax	Dinner & Relax
9 PM - 10 PM	Reading & Wind Down	Reading & Wind Down	Reading & Wind Down	Reading & Wind Down	Reading & Wind Down

Action Plan: Developing a Balanced Schedule

Step 1: Identify Your Priorities

- **Work Responsibilities:** List your key tasks and deadlines.
- **Personal Commitments:** Include family, friends, health, and hobbies.
- **Self-Care Needs:** Don't forget rest and relaxation.

Step 2: Create a Master Schedule

- **Use Tools:** Choose a planner or digital calendar that suits you.
- **Allocate Time Blocks:** Assign specific periods for each priority.
- **Be Realistic:** Ensure your schedule is achievable.

Step 3: Set Boundaries

- **Work Hours:** Define clear start and end times.
- **Personal Time:** Protect this time by avoiding work-related activities.
- **Communication:** Inform colleagues and loved ones of your availability.

Step 4: Implement Time Management Techniques

- **Prioritize Tasks:** Use the Eisenhower Matrix to focus on what's important.
- **Avoid Multitasking:** Focus on one task at a time for better efficiency.
- **Batch Similar Tasks:** Group tasks like emails and calls to streamline efforts.

Step 5: Monitor and Adjust

- **Daily Reflection:** Spend a few minutes assessing your day.
- **Weekly Review:** Adjust your schedule based on what worked and what didn't.
- **Celebrate Successes:** Acknowledge improvements, no matter how small.

Closing Thoughts

Effective time management is more than just ticking tasks off a to-do list; it's about making conscious choices that align with your values and goals. By taking control of your time, you're not just increasing productivity—you're paving the way toward a more balanced, fulfilling life.

Remember, mastering time management is a journey. It requires patience, practice, and persistence. But with each step you take, you're investing in a better version of yourself.

"The key is in not spending time, but in investing it." — Stephen R. Covey

Next Steps:

- **Implement the Time Block Challenge this week.**
- **Develop your personalized schedule using the action plan.**
- **Reflect on how these changes impact your work-life balance.**

In the next chapter, we'll explore **Setting Boundaries for Success**, focusing on how to protect your time and energy to maintain the balance you've started to create.

Chapter 4: Setting Boundaries
for Success

"Daring to set boundaries is about having the courage to love ourselves, even when we risk disappointing others." — Brené Brown

In the quest for work-life balance, setting boundaries is a powerful act of self-care and self-respect. It's not about building walls to keep people out; it's about creating space to prioritize what's truly important. Boundaries help protect your time, energy, and well-being, allowing you to thrive both professionally and personally.

In this chapter, we'll explore the importance of saying "no" to unnecessary tasks, learn how to establish and maintain healthy work boundaries, and discuss effective communication strategies to convey your limits to colleagues and supervisors. By the end, you'll be equipped with the tools to assert your needs confidently and create a balanced life that aligns with your values.

The Importance of Saying "No"

1. Understanding the Power of "No"

- **Protecting Your Time:** Every time you say "yes" to something unimportant, you're saying "no" to something that matters.
- **Preventing Burnout:** Overcommitting leads to exhaustion and decreased productivity.
- **Maintaining Focus:** Saying "no" helps you concentrate on tasks that align with your goals and values.

2. Common Reasons We Struggle to Say "No"

- **Fear of Disappointment:** Worrying about letting others down.
- **Desire to Please:** Wanting to be seen as helpful and cooperative.
- **Career Advancement Concerns:** Believing that saying "yes" to everything will lead to recognition and opportunities.

3. Reframing "No" as a Positive

- **Empowerment:** Taking control of your choices.
- **Respect:** Demonstrating self-respect and encouraging others to respect your boundaries.
- **Clarity:** Providing clear expectations about your availability and capacity.

4. Practical Strategies for Saying "No"

- **Be Polite but Firm:** Use respectful language without leaving room for ambiguity.
- **Offer Alternatives:** If appropriate, suggest another solution or timeline.
- **Practice:** The more you say "no," the more comfortable it becomes.

Setting Work Boundaries to Protect Personal Time

1. Recognizing Boundary Intrusions

- **After-Hours Work:** Responding to emails or calls during personal time.
- **Excessive Workload:** Taking on more tasks than you can handle.
- **Availability Expectations:** Feeling the need to be accessible 24/7.

2. Establishing Healthy Boundaries

- **Define Your Limits:** Know what you're willing and not willing to do.
- **Set Specific Times:** Designate work hours and personal hours.
- **Use Technology Wisely:** Turn off notifications after work hours.

3. Communicating Your Boundaries

- **Inform Colleagues:** Let your team know your availability.
- **Set Auto-Responses:** Use email or messaging apps to indicate when you're offline.

- **Lead by Example:** Respect others' boundaries to foster a supportive environment.

4. Overcoming Guilt

- **Understand Your Rights:** You're entitled to personal time without feeling guilty.
- **Focus on Benefits:** Recognize that rest improves your performance at work.
- **Seek Support:** Discuss your boundaries with trusted colleagues or mentors.

Communicating Boundaries Clearly to Colleagues and Supervisors

1. The Importance of Clear Communication

- **Avoid Misunderstandings:** Prevent confusion about your availability and commitments.
- **Build Trust:** Honesty fosters respect and reliability.
- **Enhance Professional Relationships:** Clear boundaries lead to healthier interactions.

2. Tips for Effective Communication

- **Be Direct and Respectful:** Clearly state your needs without aggression.
- **Choose the Right Time:** Discuss boundaries during appropriate moments, such as meetings or one-on-ones.
- **Provide Context:** Briefly explain why the boundary is important if necessary.

3. Sample Scripts

- **Declining Additional Tasks:**
  - "I appreciate you thinking of me for this project, but I won't be able to take it on at this time."
- **Setting Availability Limits:**
  - "I respond to emails between 8 AM and 6 PM. If something urgent comes up after that, please call me directly."
- **Requesting Support:**
  - "I've noticed my workload has increased

significantly. Can we discuss prioritizing tasks or reallocating some responsibilities?"

4. Handling Pushback

- **Stay Firm:** Politely restate your boundary if challenged.
- **Seek Compromise:** If possible, find a solution that respects your limits while addressing the other person's needs.
- **Escalate if Necessary:** If boundaries are repeatedly ignored, consider involving HR or higher management.

Checklist: Assessing Your Current Boundaries

Use this checklist to identify where your boundaries may need reinforcement:

1. **Work Intruding on Personal Time**
   - Do you check work emails or messages during personal time?
   - Have you missed personal events due to work commitments?
   - Do you feel anxious or guilty when not working?

2. **Personal Life Affecting Work**
   - Are personal issues consistently interrupting your workday?
   - Do you find it hard to focus on work due to personal distractions?
   - Are you bringing personal tasks into your work environment?

3. **Physical and Emotional Boundaries**
   - Do you feel drained because of overcommitment?
   - Are you taking on others' responsibilities regularly?
   - Do you have difficulty expressing your needs?

4. **Technology Boundaries**
   - Is your phone constantly notifying you of work-

related matters?
- Do you use the same devices for work and personal use without separation?
- Are you active on work platforms during off-hours?

Reflection:
- Identify which boundaries are being crossed most frequently.
- Consider the impact this has on your stress levels and overall well-being.
- Acknowledge areas that require immediate attention.

Exercise: Boundary Reflection

Objective: To explore an area where you struggle to set boundaries and develop strategies to strengthen them.

Instructions:

1. **Identify the Challenging Area**
   - Choose one aspect of your life where setting boundaries is difficult (e.g., responding to work emails at night, saying "yes" to every social invitation).

2. **Reflect on the Difficulty**
   - **Why is it challenging?**
     - Fear of missing out?
     - Concern about others' opinions?
     - Personal expectations?
   - **What are the consequences?**
     - Increased stress?
     - Reduced personal time?
     - Feelings of resentment?

3. **Write About It**
   - Spend 15-20 minutes journaling your thoughts.
   - Be honest and specific about your feelings and experiences.

4. **Develop Action Steps**
   - **What can you change?**
     - Set specific times to disconnect.
     - Practice saying "no" in low-stakes situations.
   - **Who can support you?**
     - Colleagues, friends, family, or a mentor.
5. **Commit to Change**
   - **Set a Goal:**
     - "I will not check work emails after 7 PM for the next two weeks."
   - **Anticipate Obstacles:**
     - Identify potential challenges and plan how to address them.

Example Entry:

- **Area of Difficulty:** Difficulty declining additional work assignments.
- **Why It's Difficult:** I worry that saying "no" will make me seem uncommitted or harm my chances for promotion.
- **Consequences:** I'm overwhelmed, my work quality is slipping, and I have no time for myself.
- **Action Steps:** Discuss workload with my supervisor, prioritize tasks, and practice polite ways to decline extra work.

Action Plan: Setting Three Non-Negotiable Boundaries

Objective: Establish firm boundaries to protect your well-being and support work-life balance.

Steps:

1. **Identify Your Non-Negotiables**
   - **Boundary 1:** *(e.g., No work emails after 7 PM)*
   - **Boundary 2:** *(e.g., Reserve Sundays for family time)*
   - **Boundary 3:** *(e.g., Take a 30-minute lunch break away from the desk each day)*
2. **Implement the Boundaries**

- **Communicate Clearly:**
    - Inform relevant parties of your new boundaries.
    - Use tools like calendar blocks or auto-replies.
- **Set Reminders:**
    - Use alarms or notifications to reinforce new habits.
- **Adjust Environment:**
    - Remove work apps from personal devices if necessary.
    - Create physical spaces dedicated to relaxation.

3. **Monitor Your Progress**
   - **Keep a Journal:**
       - Note any challenges or successes in adhering to your boundaries.
   - **Assess Impact:**
       - Observe changes in stress levels, productivity, and personal satisfaction.

4. **Maintain Accountability**
   - **Involve Others:**
       - Share your goals with a trusted friend or colleague who can offer support.
   - **Regular Check-Ins:**
       - Schedule time to review your boundaries and adjust as needed.

5. **Evaluate After One Month**
   - **Reflect on Outcomes:**
       - Have these boundaries improved your work-life balance?
       - What benefits have you noticed?
   - **Decide on Next Steps:**
       - Continue with existing boundaries, adjust them, or add new ones.

Example Action Plan:

- **Boundary 1:** No work communication after 6 PM.
  - **Implementation:** Turn off work email notifications; inform team of availability.
- **Boundary 2:** Dedicated exercise time every morning.
  - **Implementation:** Block time on calendar; prepare gym clothes the night before.
- **Boundary 3:** Do not accept new tasks without assessing current workload.
    - **Implementation:** Pause before responding to requests; use a task management tool to visualize commitments.

Closing Thoughts

Setting boundaries is a vital practice for achieving and maintaining work-life balance. It's an act of self-respect that enables you to preserve your energy for the things that truly matter. Remember, boundaries are not about isolation but about creating a healthy space where you can flourish.

By saying "no" to what doesn't serve you, you open doors to opportunities that align with your values and goals. Communicating your boundaries clearly and confidently fosters mutual respect and understanding in your professional and personal relationships.

.

"You get what you tolerate." — *Henry Cloud*

It's time to stop tolerating the erosion of your personal time and start building the balanced life you deserve.

Next Steps:

- **Complete the Boundary Reflection Exercise.**
- **Implement your three non-negotiable boundaries starting this week.**
- **Observe the changes in your stress levels and overall**

happiness.

In the next chapter, we'll delve into **Building Healthy Habits for the Long Term**, exploring how consistent practices can support sustained balance and personal growth.

Midway Reflection: A Journey of Discovery

An Odyssey to the Far East

"Not all those who wander are lost." —*J.R.R. Tolkien*

Several years ago, I found myself standing atop a serene hill in a small village in the Far East, gazing at a sunrise that painted the sky with hues of gold and crimson. The air was crisp, carrying the subtle scent of cherry blossoms, and the distant sound of a temple bell resonated through the valley. I had embarked on this journey seeking something intangible—perhaps inspiration, clarity, or a new perspective on life that seemed elusive amidst the hustle and bustle of my daily routine.

Back home, life was a whirlwind of meetings, deadlines, and an ever-growing to-do list. I was chasing success but felt like I was running in circles. The more I achieved, the more hollow the victories seemed. There was a constant pressure to do more, be more, and give more, yet I felt disconnected from myself and the world around me.

In the Far East, I immersed myself in cultures that valued balance, mindfulness, and harmony. I spent time with a wise monk who told me, "A fulfilled life is not measured by how much we do, but by how deeply we experience each moment." Those words struck a chord deep within me. I realized that in my pursuit of success, I had neglected the essence of living—a harmonious balance between doing and being.

I practiced meditation, learned about the principles of yin and yang, and embraced the simplicity of daily rituals that honored both work and rest. This journey was not just across continents but into the depths of my own soul. It was a transformative experience that ignited a desire to share these insights with others facing similar struggles.

The Inspiration Behind This Book

Returning home, I saw my life—and the lives of those around me —with new eyes. Friends and colleagues were caught in the same cycle I had been in, striving relentlessly yet feeling unfulfilled. The modern world seemed to glorify overachievement, equating nonstop productivity with worthiness. But at what cost?

I felt a calling to write this book, to serve as a guide for young professionals navigating the complexities of contemporary life. My goal was to blend practical strategies with heartfelt reflections, offering a roadmap to achieve not just professional success but a fulfilling, balanced life.

I wanted to share the lessons learned from my journey:

- **The importance of self-awareness:** Understanding who we are beyond our titles and accomplishments.
- **The power of intentional living:** Making conscious choices that align with our core values.
- **The necessity of balance:** Recognizing that rest and play are just as vital as work.

This book is a culmination of personal experiences, insights from thought leaders, and actionable steps designed to empower you to create a life that resonates with your true self.

A Generation of Overachievers

"We are human beings, not human doings." — Anonymous

Our generation has been conditioned to believe that success is defined by how much we can accomplish in the shortest amount of time. The advent of technology has blurred the lines between work and personal life, making it harder to unplug and just be. Social media bombards us with highlight reels of others' achievements, fueling a perpetual race to outdo not only others but ourselves.

This relentless pursuit often leads to:

- **Burnout:** Physical and emotional exhaustion from prolonged stress.
- **Loss of Identity:** Defining ourselves solely by our careers

or achievements.

- **Disconnected Relationships:** Neglecting personal connections due to work demands.

It's time to challenge this narrative. Success should not come at the expense of our health, happiness, or relationships. By redefining what success means to us individually, we can break free from societal pressures and create a more balanced, fulfilling life.

Reflection on Our Journey So Far

As we reach the halfway point of this book, let's take a moment to reflect on the ground we've covered:

- **Chapter 1: Understanding the Imbalance**
  - We identified the signs of imbalance in our lives and acknowledged the toll it takes on our well-being.
  - We challenged the myth of hustle culture and began to redefine success on our own terms.
- **Chapter 2: Defining Your Core Values**
  - We delved into self-discovery to uncover what truly matters to us.
  - We learned how aligning our actions with our core values leads to a more authentic and satisfying life.
- **Chapter 3: The Power of Time Management**
  - We explored techniques to manage our most precious resource—time.
  - We implemented tools like the Eisenhower Matrix to prioritize tasks effectively.
- **Chapter 4: Setting Boundaries for Success**
  - We recognized the importance of saying "no" and setting healthy boundaries.
  - We developed strategies to protect our personal time and communicated our limits to others.

Through these chapters, we've built a foundation for achieving work-life balance. Each step has been about empowering you to take control, make intentional choices, and create a life that reflects your true self.

What Lies Ahead

The journey doesn't end here. The upcoming chapters will delve deeper into sustaining the balance you've begun to establish:

- **Chapter 5: Building Healthy Habits for the Long Term**
    - We'll discuss how to cultivate habits that support your well-being and long-term goals.
    - You'll learn about the science of habit formation and how to make lasting changes.
- **Chapter 6: Managing Stress and Avoiding Burnout**
    - We'll address the realities of stress in our lives and provide practical techniques to manage it.
    - You'll discover ways to recognize early signs of burnout and strategies to prevent it.
- **Chapter 7: Cultivating a Support System**
    - We'll explore the significance of nurturing relationships that uplift and support you.
    - You'll learn how to build a network that encourages balance and personal growth.
- **Chapter 8: Sustaining Balance and Moving Forward**
    - We'll tie all the concepts together, focusing on maintaining balance amid life's inevitable changes.
    - You'll create a personalized plan to carry these principles into the future.

Closing Thoughts

"The longest journey you will make in your life is from your head to your heart." — Sioux Legend

As we move forward, keep in mind that seeking balance is

a courageous act in a world that often pulls us in opposing directions. It's a journey worth taking—a journey back to yourself.

Thank you for allowing me to be a part of your path. Let's continue this exploration together, with curiosity, compassion, and a commitment to living authentically.

Next Steps:

- **Reflect on Your Own Journey:** Consider how the themes discussed so far resonate with your experiences.
- **Reconnect with Your Purpose:** Remind yourself why achieving balance is important to you.
- **Prepare for What's Ahead:** Approach the upcoming chapters with an open mind and a willingness to grow.

Together, we'll continue to build the life you envision—one of balance, fulfillment, and true success..

Chapter 5: Building Healthy Habits for the Long Term

Introduction

"We are what we repeatedly do. Excellence, then, is not an act, but a habit." — Aristotle

In our journey toward achieving work-life balance, the habits we cultivate play a pivotal role. Habits are the building blocks of our daily lives, the routines that shape our actions, thoughts, and ultimately, our destiny. By developing healthy habits, we create a foundation that supports not just our professional success but our overall well-being.

In this chapter, we'll explore the profound impact of habits on maintaining balance. We'll delve into the science of habit formation, understanding how small daily actions can either enhance or disrupt our work-life harmony. Adopting a holistic view, we'll consider the interconnectedness of our physical, mental, and emotional health, recognizing that true balance encompasses all aspects of our being.

The Role of Habits in Maintaining Balance

1. Understanding Habits as Foundations

- **Habits Shape Our Lives:** They determine how we spend our time, how we react to situations, and how we pursue our goals.
- **Automatic Behaviors:** Habits are actions we perform with little conscious thought, freeing mental energy for other tasks.
- **Influence on Well-Being:** Positive habits contribute to health and happiness, while negative ones can hinder our progress.

2. The Holistic Impact of Habits

- **Physical Health:** Regular exercise, nutritious eating, and

adequate sleep enhance our energy levels and resilience.
- **Mental and Emotional Health:** Mindfulness practices, gratitude journaling, and positive affirmations support mental clarity and emotional stability.
- **Spiritual Well-Being:** Engaging in activities that nurture your spirit—such as meditation, nature walks, or community service—fosters a sense of purpose and connection.

3. Habits as Tools for Balance

- **Consistency Over Intensity:** Small, consistent actions often lead to more sustainable results than sporadic, intense efforts.
- **Integration into Daily Life:** Embedding healthy habits into your routine ensures they become a natural part of your lifestyle.
- **Alignment with Values:** Habits that reflect your core values strengthen your commitment to them, enhancing overall harmony.

How Small Daily Habits Enhance or Disrupt Work-Life Harmony

1. The Cumulative Effect of Small Actions

- **Positive Ripple Effect:** Simple habits like starting the day with a healthy breakfast or a short meditation can set a positive tone for the day.
- **Negative Patterns:** Seemingly minor habits, such as checking emails first thing in the morning or skipping meals, can accumulate and lead to imbalance.

2. Examples of Enhancing Habits

- **Morning Rituals:** Establishing a morning routine that centers you—such as stretching, journaling, or mindful breathing.
- **Mindful Breaks:** Taking short pauses throughout the day to refocus and recharge.
- **Intentional Disconnecting:** Setting aside time to unplug

from technology and engage in restorative activities.

3. Examples of Disruptive Habits

- **Overworking:** Habitually extending work hours into personal time erodes boundaries.
- **Neglecting Self-Care:** Ignoring signs of fatigue or stress can lead to burnout.
- **Unhealthy Coping Mechanisms:** Relying on substances or excessive screen time to unwind may provide temporary relief but harm long-term well-being.

4. Holistic Habit Integration

- **Body-Mind Connection:** Recognizing that physical health influences mental clarity and emotional stability.
- **Emotional Awareness:** Developing habits that promote emotional intelligence, such as reflective journaling or open communication.
- **Environmental Influence:** Creating spaces that support healthy habits—organizing your workspace, cultivating a peaceful home environment.

The Science of Habit Formation: The Cue-Routine-Reward Cycle

1. Understanding the Habit Loop

- **Cue:** A trigger that tells your brain to initiate a behavior.
- **Routine:** The behavior itself, which can be physical, mental, or emotional.
- **Reward:** The positive reinforcement that tells your brain the routine is worthwhile.

2. How Habits Are Formed

- **Neurological Pathways:** Repetition strengthens neural connections, making the habit more automatic.
- **Craving the Reward:** Anticipation of the reward reinforces the habit loop.

3. Strategies for Building New Habits

- **Identify Cues:** Use existing routines as triggers for

new habits (e.g., after brushing teeth, meditate for five minutes).

- **Define Clear Routines:** Specify the behavior you want to adopt in detail.
- **Establish Rewards:** Choose meaningful rewards that reinforce the habit (e.g., enjoying a piece of fruit after a workout).

4. Breaking Unhealthy Habits

- **Recognize Triggers:** Identify what prompts the undesirable habit.
- **Substitute Routines:** Replace the negative behavior with a positive one that satisfies the same need.
- **Adjust Rewards:** Find healthier rewards that provide similar satisfaction.

Checklist: Assessing Your Current Habits

Use this checklist to evaluate the habits that dominate your daily life:

1. **Morning Routine**
   - Do you start your day feeling rushed or calm?
   - Are you engaging in activities that energize you?

2. **Work Habits**
   - Do you take regular breaks to avoid burnout?
   - Are you prioritizing tasks effectively or frequently multitasking?

3. **Eating and Exercise**
   - Are you consuming nutritious meals regularly?
   - Do you incorporate physical activity into your routine?

4. **Technology Use**
   - How much time do you spend on screens outside of work?
   - Do you check work emails during personal time?

5. **Evening Routine**

- Do you have a winding-down ritual to promote restful sleep?
- Are you getting sufficient sleep consistently?

6. **Emotional Well-Being**
   - Do you practice stress-reduction techniques?
   - Are you aware of and processing your emotions constructively?

Reflection:

- **Alignment with Balance:** Identify which habits support your work-life harmony and which disrupt it.
- **Areas for Improvement:** Note any habits you'd like to change or develop.

Exercise: Habit Tracker

Objective: Cultivate a positive habit over 30 days to enhance your well-being and contribute to balance.

Instructions:

1. **Choose One Positive Habit**
   - Examples: Daily exercise, morning meditation, reading before bed, practicing gratitude.

2. **Set Clear Parameters**
   - **Specificity:** Define the habit in precise terms (e.g., "Meditate for 10 minutes each morning after waking up").
   - **Achievability:** Ensure it's realistic within your current lifestyle.

3. **Create a Tracking Method**
   - Use a journal, calendar, or habit-tracking app.
   - Mark each day you successfully perform the habit.

4. **Establish Reminders and Cues**
   - Set alarms or place visual cues where you'll see them.

5. **Reflect Weekly**
- Note any challenges, successes, and how the habit affects your overall balance.

6. **Adjust as Needed**
- If obstacles arise, modify the habit to maintain consistency.

Example Habit Tracker Template:

Day	Completed?	Notes
1	Yes	Felt more focused today.
2	Yes	Slightly rushed but did it.
...	...	...
30		

Action Plan: Developing Holistic Habits for Lasting Balance

Step 1: Identify Two Habits To Improve

- **Work-Related Habit:**
    - *Example:* Reducing multitasking by focusing on one task at a time.
- **Personal-Life Habit:**
    - *Example:* Incorporating daily mindfulness meditation.

Step 2: Set Clear Goals and Timelines
- **Work Habit Goal:**
    - **Specific Goal:** Allocate dedicated time blocks for individual tasks without interruptions.
    - **Timeline:** Implement over the next four weeks, gradually increasing focus periods.
- **Personal Habit Goal:**
    - **Specific Goal:** Meditate for 10 minutes each evening before bed.
    - **Timeline:** Start tonight and continue daily for the next 30 days.

Step 3: Embrace a Holistic Approach
- **Integrate Mind and Body:**
    - Recognize how improving your work habit can reduce stress, enhancing physical health.
    - Understand that personal habits like meditation improve mental clarity, benefiting professional performance.
- **Consider Environmental Factors:**
    - **Workspace:** Organize your work area to minimize distractions.
    - **Home Environment:** Create a calming space for personal practices.

Step 4: Implement and Monitor Progress
- **Use Habit Tracking Tools:**
    - Continue using the Habit Tracker for both habits.

- Note correlations between habits and overall well-being.
  - **Seek Support:**
    - Share your goals with a colleague or friend who can encourage you.
    - Consider joining a community or group with similar objectives.

Step 5: Reflect and Adjust
  - **Regular Reflection:**
    - Set aside time each week to assess how the habits are affecting your balance.
    - Celebrate successes and identify areas needing adjustment.

  - **Long-Term Vision:**
    - Envision how maintaining these habits contributes to your overall life goals.
    - Stay flexible and open to evolving your habits as you grow.

Closing Thoughts

Building healthy habits is a journey of self-discovery and commitment. By adopting a holistic perspective, you acknowledge that every aspect of your life is interconnected. The habits you cultivate in your personal life influence your professional performance and vice versa.

Remember, lasting change doesn't happen overnight. It requires patience, consistency, and compassion toward yourself. Embrace the process, knowing that each small step brings you closer to a balanced and fulfilling life.

"First we make our habits, then our habits make us." —*John Dryden*

Next Steps:

- **Start Your Habit Tracker Today:** Choose your positive habit and begin tracking.

- **Implement Your Action Plan:** Set clear goals for your work-related and personal-life habits.
- **Adopt a Holistic Mindset:** Consider how your habits affect all areas of your well-being.

In the next chapter, we'll explore **Managing Stress and Avoiding Burnout**, incorporating a holistic approach to understand and address the multifaceted nature of stress in our lives.

Chapter 6: Managing Stress and Avoiding Burnout

"The greatest weapon against stress is our ability to choose one thought over another." — William James

In the relentless pace of modern life, stress has become an almost constant companion for many young professionals. While a certain level of stress can motivate us to perform, chronic stress can lead to burnout—a state of physical, emotional, and mental exhaustion. Recognizing the signs early and adopting effective stress management techniques are crucial for maintaining the balance we've been striving to achieve.

In this chapter, we'll explore how to identify the signs of stress and burnout before they take a toll on your well-being. We'll delve into practical, holistic stress management techniques, drawing inspiration from both Western practices and the ancient wisdom of India. By embracing a comprehensive approach that nurtures the mind, body, and spirit, you'll be better equipped to handle setbacks and tough days without losing your balance.

Identifying the Signs of Stress and Burnout Before It's Too Late

1. Understanding Stress and Burnout

- **Stress:** A natural response to challenging situations, which can be positive (eustress) or negative (distress).
- **Burnout:** A state of chronic stress leading to physical and emotional exhaustion, cynicism, detachment, and feelings of ineffectiveness.

2. Common Signs of Stress

- **Physical Symptoms:** Headaches, muscle tension, sleep disturbances, fatigue.
- **Emotional Symptoms:** Anxiety, irritability, restlessness, feelings of overwhelm.
- **Behavioral Symptoms:** Changes in appetite, procrastination, increased use of alcohol or drugs.

3. Recognizing Burnout Indicators

- **Chronic Fatigue:** Feeling tired most days, even after rest.
- **Lack of Motivation:** Difficulty starting tasks or a sense of dread about work.
- **Cynicism and Detachment:** Feeling disconnected from work and colleagues.
- **Decreased Performance:** Reduced productivity and inability to concentrate.

4. Holistic Perspective on Stress

- **Interconnectedness:** Stress affects not just the mind but the body and spirit.
- **Balance Disruption:** Prolonged stress disrupts the harmony between different aspects of your being.
- **Early Detection:** Being mindful of subtle changes helps prevent escalation.

5. The Importance of Self-Awareness

- **Mindfulness Practices:** Regularly checking in with yourself to assess your mental and emotional state.
- **Journaling:** Recording thoughts and feelings to identify patterns over time.
- **Seeking Feedback:** Trusted friends or mentors can provide insights you might overlook.

Practical Stress Management Techniques

1. Mindfulness Meditation

- **What It Is:** A practice of focusing your attention on the present moment without judgment.
- **Benefits:** Reduces anxiety, enhances emotional regulation, and improves overall well-being.
- **How to Practice:**
  - **Find a Quiet Space:** Sit comfortably with your back straight.
  - **Focus on Your Breath:** Observe the sensation of breathing in and out.
  - **Acknowledge Thoughts:** Notice when your

mind wanders and gently bring it back to the breath.

2. Breathing Exercises (Pranayama)

Drawing from ancient Indian practices, pranayama involves controlling the breath to influence the flow of life force (prana) in the body.

- **Deep Belly Breathing:**
    - **Technique:** Inhale slowly through the nose, allowing the abdomen to expand; exhale through the mouth.
    - **Benefits:** Activates the parasympathetic nervous system, promoting relaxation.
- **Alternate Nostril Breathing (Nadi Shodhana):**
    - **Technique:** Use your right thumb to close your right nostril; inhale through the left nostril. Close the left nostril with your ring finger; exhale through the right nostril. Inhale through the right nostril, close it, and exhale through the left.
    - **Benefits:** Balances the left and right hemispheres of the brain, reduces stress, and enhances mental clarity.

3. Yoga and Physical Movement

- **Yoga Asanas (Postures):** Combining physical poses with breath control and meditation.
    - **Benefits:** Improves flexibility, strength, and reduces stress.
    - **Recommended Poses:**
        - **Child's Pose (Balasana):** Promotes relaxation and relieves tension in the back.
        - **Standing Forward Bend (Uttanasana):** Calms the mind and stretches the hamstrings.
        - **Legs Up the Wall Pose (Viparita Karani):** Reduces anxiety and promotes circulation.
- **Walking or Tai Chi:** Gentle movements that connect

body and mind.

4. Short Breaks and Micro-Restoration

- **Pomodoro Technique:** Work in focused intervals (e.g., 25 minutes) followed by short breaks (5 minutes).
- **Mindful Pauses:** Take a few moments throughout the day to stretch, breathe deeply, or gaze out a window.
- **Digital Detox Moments:** Step away from screens periodically to reduce cognitive load.

5. Ayurveda and Holistic Health

Ayurveda, the traditional Indian system of medicine, emphasizes balance among the body's energies (doshas).

- **Diet and Nutrition:**
    - **Balanced Meals:** Incorporate all six tastes (sweet, sour, salty, bitter, pungent, astringent) to satisfy the palate and nourish the body.
    - **Herbal Teas:** Chamomile, ashwagandha, or tulsi (holy basil) teas can soothe the nervous system.
- **Daily Routine (Dinacharya):**
    - **Consistent Schedule:** Wake up and go to bed at the same times each day.
    - **Self-Massage (Abhyanga):** Applying warm oil to the body can calm the mind and promote circulation.

6. Cultivating a Positive Mindset

- **Gratitude Practice:** Regularly acknowledging what you're thankful for enhances emotional resilience.
- **Affirmations:** Positive statements that reinforce desired beliefs and attitudes.
- **Connecting with Nature:** Spending time outdoors to ground yourself and gain perspective.

How to Handle Setbacks and Tough Days Without Losing Balance

1. Acceptance and Mindfulness

- **Acknowledge Emotions:** Allow yourself to feel without judgment.

- **Stay Present:** Focus on the current moment rather than dwelling on the past or worrying about the future.

2. Reframing Challenges

- **Growth Mindset:** View setbacks as opportunities to learn and grow.
- **Perspective Taking:** Consider how this challenge fits into the bigger picture.

3. Self-Compassion

- **Be Kind to Yourself:** Treat yourself with the same understanding you would offer a friend.
- **Avoid Negative Self-Talk:** Replace self-criticism with supportive language.

4. Seek Support

- **Connect with Others:** Share your experiences with trusted friends, family, or colleagues.
- **Professional Help:** Consider speaking with a counselor or therapist if needed.

5. Maintain Routine and Self-Care

- **Stick to Healthy Habits:** Continue practices that support your well-being.
- **Prioritize Rest:** Ensure you're getting adequate sleep and relaxation.

Checklist: Are You Experiencing Burnout?

Use this checklist to evaluate your current state:

1. **Physical Symptoms:**
   - Do you frequently feel tired or drained?
   - Are you experiencing headaches, muscle pain, or changes in appetite?

2. **Emotional Indicators:**
   - Do you feel detached or alone in the world?
   - Are you experiencing feelings of self-doubt or failure?

3. **Behavioral Signs:**
   - Have you become cynical or critical at work?
   - Are you using food, drugs, or alcohol to cope?

4. **Work Performance:**
   - Is your productivity declining?
   - Do you have trouble concentrating?

5. **Motivation and Satisfaction:**
   - Do you lack motivation to engage in work or personal activities?
   - Are you feeling a decreased sense of accomplishment?

Reflection:

- **Total Yes Responses:**
  - 0-2: You're likely managing stress well.
  - 3-5: Be cautious; consider implementing stress management strategies.
  - 6 or more: You may be experiencing burnout and should take immediate action.

Exercise: Stress Reflection

Objective: Increase awareness of your stress responses and identify healthier coping strategies.

Instructions:

1. **Recall a Recent Stressful Event**
   - Choose an incident that caused significant stress.

2. **Reflect on Your Response**
   - **Emotions Felt:** What emotions did you experience (e.g., anger, frustration, sadness)?
   - **Physical Reactions:** Notice any bodily sensations (e.g., tension, rapid heartbeat).
   - **Actions Taken:** How did you respond? Did you withdraw, confront, or avoid the situation?

3. **Evaluate the Outcome**
   - **Effectiveness:** Did your response resolve the

situation or alleviate stress?

· **Impact on Well-Being:** How did it affect your mood and energy levels afterward?

4. **Identify Alternative Strategies**
   · **What Could You Do Differently?**
     · Could you have communicated your feelings more effectively?
     · Might taking a short break have helped?

5. **Plan for Future Situations**
   · **Implement New Techniques:** Decide on a strategy to use next time a similar situation arises.
   · **Practice Skills:** If needed, rehearse mindfulness or communication techniques.

Example Entry:

· **Event:** Tight deadline at work caused me to work late hours.
· **Response:** Felt anxious and irritable; skipped meals; snapped at a colleague.
· **Outcome:** Met the deadline but felt exhausted and guilty for my behavior.
· **Alternative Strategies:** Next time, I will communicate workload concerns to my supervisor and take short breaks to recharge.
· **Plan:** Practice deep breathing exercises when feeling overwhelmed.

Action Plan: Create a Personalized Stress-Relief Toolkit

Objective: Develop a set of quick, actionable strategies to manage stress effectively.

Steps:

1. **List 5 Quick Stress-Relief Techniques**
   · **Technique 1: Deep Breathing Exercises**
     · Practice diaphragmatic breathing for 5

minutes.

- **Technique 2: Mindful Walking**
  - Take a 10-minute walk outdoors, focusing on the sensations.
- **Technique 3: Progressive Muscle Relaxation**
  - Tense and relax muscle groups to reduce physical tension.
- **Technique 4: Aromatherapy**
  - Use essential oils like lavender or eucalyptus to promote calmness.
- **Technique 5: Expressive Writing**
  - Spend 15 minutes journaling thoughts and feelings.

2. **Gather Necessary Resources**
   - **Breathing App:** Download a guided breathing app.
   - **Comfortable Shoes:** Keep them handy for walks.
   - **Essential Oils:** Purchase a small diffuser or scented oils.
   - **Journal and Pen:** Keep them accessible for writing exercises.

3. **Implement Techniques as Needed**
   - Recognize early signs of stress and choose an appropriate technique.
   - Rotate strategies to find what works best in different situations.

4. **Incorporate Techniques into Daily Routine**
   - **Morning Ritual:** Begin the day with deep breathing or meditation.
   - **Work Breaks:** Use mindful walking or stretching during breaks.
   - **Evening Wind-Down:** Practice progressive muscle relaxation before bed.

5. **Evaluate and Adjust**
   - **Reflection:** Note which techniques are most

effective.
- **Adaptation:** Modify or add new strategies as needed.

Holistic and Indian Perspectives on Stress Management

1. Embracing a Holistic Approach

- **Mind-Body-Spirit Connection:** Recognize that true wellness involves balancing all aspects of yourself.
- **Integration of Practices:** Combine physical activities, mental exercises, and spiritual reflections.

2. Wisdom from Indian Traditions

- **Ayurvedic Principles:**
  - **Dosha Balance:** Understand your body type (Vata, Pitta, Kapha) and adopt lifestyle choices that promote harmony.
  - **Herbal Remedies:** Incorporate herbs like ashwagandha for stress relief under professional guidance.
- **Yoga Philosophy:**
  - **Eight Limbs of Yoga:** Beyond physical postures, yoga includes ethical guidelines, breath control, and meditation.
  - **Karma Yoga:** The path of selfless action can reduce stress by focusing on service without attachment to outcomes.
- **Meditation Techniques:**
  - **Transcendental Meditation:** A mantra-based practice that promotes deep relaxation.
  - **Loving-Kindness Meditation (Metta):** Cultivates compassion for self and others.

3. Cultural Practices for Stress Relief

- **Art and Music Therapy:**
  - **Classical Indian Music:** Listening to soothing ragas can calm the mind.
  - **Mandala Coloring:** Engaging in intricate designs aids concentration and relaxation.
- **Community and Connection:**

- **Satsang:** Gathering with like-minded individuals for spiritual discourse.
- **Festivals and Rituals:** Participating in cultural celebrations fosters joy and a sense of belonging.

Closing Thoughts

"When meditation is mastered, the mind is unwavering like the flame of a lamp in a windless place." — *Bhagavad Gita*

Managing stress and avoiding burnout are essential components of sustaining the balance you've worked hard to achieve. By integrating practical techniques with a holistic understanding of well-being, you equip yourself to navigate life's challenges with grace and resilience.

Drawing inspiration from both modern practices and ancient wisdom, you can create a personalized approach that resonates with your unique needs. Remember that seeking balance is a continuous journey, one that invites you to be compassionate with yourself and open to growth.

As you continue on this path, know that each step you take toward managing stress not only enhances your own life but also positively impacts those around you.

Next Steps:

- **Complete the Stress Reflection Exercise.**
- **Assemble Your Personalized Stress-Relief Toolkit and begin implementing the techniques.**
- **Embrace a Holistic Perspective:** Consider how integrating mind, body, and spirit practices enhances your well-being.

In the next chapter, we'll explore **Cultivating a Support System**, understanding the importance of relationships and community in maintaining work-life balance.

Chapter 7: Cultivating a Support System

"If you want to go fast, go alone. If you want to go far, go together." — *African Proverb*

In our pursuit of work-life balance, we often focus on personal strategies and self-improvement techniques. While individual efforts are crucial, the journey toward a balanced life doesn't have to be a solitary one. Cultivating a strong support system is an essential component that can enrich your experiences, provide encouragement during challenging times, and celebrate your successes along the way.

In this chapter, we'll explore the vital role relationships play in maintaining balance. We'll delve into ways to find and nurture meaningful connections both at work and in your personal life. By building a network of mentors, friends, family, and like-minded individuals, you'll create a supportive environment that not only aids in achieving balance but also enhances your overall well-being.

The Role of Relationships in Maintaining Balance

1. Understanding the Importance of Connections

- **Emotional Support:** Relationships provide a safety net during stressful times, offering comfort and understanding.
- **Accountability Partners:** Trusted individuals can help you stay committed to your goals and remind you of your priorities.
- **Shared Experiences:** Connecting with others who are on a similar journey can foster a sense of belonging and reduce feelings of isolation.
- **Resource Sharing:** Friends and colleagues can offer valuable insights, advice, and opportunities that you might not discover on your own.

2. The Impact of Social Support on Well-Being

- **Physical Health Benefits:** Strong social ties are linked to lower stress levels, improved immune function, and increased longevity.
- **Mental Health Advantages:** Positive relationships can reduce anxiety and depression, enhancing overall happiness.
- **Work Satisfaction:** Supportive colleagues and mentors contribute to a more fulfilling and productive work environment.

3. Holistic Perspective on Relationships

- **Mind-Body Connection:** Nurturing relationships satisfies fundamental human needs for connection, impacting both mental and physical health.
- **Spiritual Growth:** Engaging with others can provide opportunities for empathy, compassion, and personal growth.
- **Balance Reinforcement:** Surrounding yourself with people who value balance encourages you to maintain your commitments to yourself.

Finding and Nurturing Meaningful Connections

1. Building Relationships at Work

- **Identify Allies:** Seek out colleagues who share similar values and work ethics.
- **Engage in Open Communication:** Foster transparency and trust by sharing your goals and challenges.
- **Participate in Team Activities:** Join committees, projects, or social events to connect with others beyond daily tasks.
- **Offer Support:** Be willing to help others, which can strengthen bonds and encourage reciprocity.

2. Enhancing Personal Life Connections

- **Reconnect with Loved Ones:** Make time for family and

friends you may have lost touch with due to work commitments.

- **Join Clubs or Groups:** Engage in community organizations, hobby groups, or volunteer opportunities that align with your interests.
- **Cultivate New Friendships:** Be open to meeting new people through social events, workshops, or networking opportunities.
- **Prioritize Quality Time:** Dedicate uninterrupted time to nurture relationships, focusing on presence and genuine interaction.

3. Seeking Mentors and Role Models

- **Identify Potential Mentors:** Look for individuals whose careers and lifestyles you admire.
- **Initiate Contact:** Reach out respectfully, expressing your interest in learning from them.
- **Establish Mutual Expectations:** Clarify how often you'll communicate and what you hope to gain from the relationship.
- **Be Receptive and Grateful:** Show appreciation for their time and insights, and be open to feedback.

4. Nurturing Relationships Through Technology

- **Stay Connected Virtually:** Use video calls, messaging apps, or social media to maintain relationships, especially if distance is a factor.
- **Create Online Communities:** Join or form groups centered around shared interests or goals.
- **Balance Screen Time:** Ensure that virtual interactions complement, rather than replace, in-person connections when possible.

Building a Support Network to Help Maintain Balance

1. Assessing Your Current Network

- **Diversity of Support:** Aim for a mix of personal and

professional relationships.

- **Alignment with Values:** Surround yourself with people who respect and support your commitment to balance.
- **Positive Influence:** Choose relationships that uplift and encourage your growth.

2. Strategies for Strengthening Your Support System

- **Regular Check-Ins:** Schedule consistent times to connect with key individuals.
- **Shared Activities:** Engage in hobbies or interests together to deepen bonds.
- **Open Dialogue:** Communicate your needs and listen actively to others.
- **Celebrate Successes:** Acknowledge and celebrate milestones, both theirs and yours.

3. Setting Boundaries Within Relationships

- **Respect Personal Space:** Recognize when you or others need time alone to recharge.
- **Communicate Limits:** Be honest about your availability and commitments.
- **Healthy Expectations:** Understand that no single person can meet all your needs; cultivate a network to provide balanced support.

4. Overcoming Challenges in Relationships

- **Addressing Conflict:** Approach disagreements with empathy and a willingness to understand.
- **Letting Go of Toxic Relationships:** Recognize when a relationship is consistently draining or harmful, and consider distancing yourself.
- **Seeking Professional Help:** If relationship issues persist, consider counseling or therapy to navigate complexities.

Checklist: Assessing the Strength of Your Support System

Use the following questions to evaluate your current support network:

1. **Variety of Connections:**
   - Do you have friends both within and outside of work?
   - Are there mentors or role models you can turn to for guidance?

2. **Encouragement and Accountability:**
   - Do your relationships motivate you to maintain work-life balance?
   - Are there people who hold you accountable to your goals?

3. **Emotional Support:**
   - Can you openly share your feelings and challenges with someone?
   - Do you feel heard and understood by your close connections?

4. **Positive Influence:**
   - Are you surrounded by individuals who exhibit balanced lifestyles?
   - Do your relationships inspire personal and professional growth?

5. **Reciprocity:**
   - Is there a mutual give-and-take in your relationships?
   - Do you feel comfortable both offering and receiving support?

6. **Impact on Well-Being:**
   - Do certain relationships consistently cause stress or drain your energy?
   - Are you able to set boundaries without fear of damaging the relationship?

Reflection:

- **Strengths:** Identify areas where your support system is strong.
- **Areas for Improvement:** Note any gaps or relationships

that may need attention.

- **Action Steps:** Consider specific ways to enhance your network.

Exercise: Relationship Audit

Objective: Gain clarity on how your relationships affect your work-life balance and identify steps to strengthen positive connections.

Instructions:

1. **List Your Closest Relationships**
   - Include family members, friends, colleagues, mentors, and any significant connections.

2. **Assess Each Relationship**

For each person, consider the following:

- **Contribution to Balance:**
  - Do they support your efforts to maintain balance?
  - Do they respect your boundaries and commitments?
- **Emotional Impact:**
  - How do you feel after interacting with them? Energized, neutral, or drained?
- **Communication Quality:**
  - Are your interactions open and honest?
  - Do you feel comfortable discussing important matters?

3. **Identify Relationships that Bring Stress**
   - Note any individuals who consistently contribute to stress or imbalance.
   - Reflect on the reasons why and whether the issues can be addressed.

4. **Plan to Strengthen Positive Relationships**
   - **Enhance Communication:**
     - Schedule regular catch-ups or share

more about your journey toward balance.
- **Express Appreciation:**
    - Acknowledge their support and let them know their importance in your life.
- **Engage in Shared Activities:**
    - Find common interests to enjoy together.

5. **Address Challenging Relationships**
- **Open Dialogue:**
    - Consider having a constructive conversation about any issues.
- **Set Boundaries:**
    - Clearly define what you are comfortable with in the relationship.
- **Evaluate the Relationship:**
    - Decide if it's beneficial to continue the relationship as it is, make changes, or distance yourself.

Example Entry:

- **Person:** Sarah (Colleague)
    - **Contribution to Balance:** Often encourages me to take breaks and respects my boundaries.
    - **Emotional Impact:** Feel supported and understood after our interactions.
    - **Action Plan:** Continue to collaborate on projects and express gratitude for her support.

- **Person:** Mike (Friend)
    - **Contribution to Balance:** Frequently asks me to work overtime with him; dismisses my need for personal time.
    - **Emotional Impact:** Feel pressured and drained.
    - **Action Plan:** Have an open conversation about my commitment to balance; set clear boundaries regarding work and personal time.

Action Plan: Strengthening Your Support System

Step 1: Plan Regular Check-Ins

- **Schedule Consistent Times:**
    - Set up weekly or monthly meetings or calls with key individuals.
- **Use Technology Wisely:**
    - Utilize calendars, reminders, or apps to keep track of appointments.
- **Be Flexible:**
    - Adjust frequency and timing as needed to accommodate both parties.

Step 2: Communicate Openly
- **Share Your Goals:**
    - Let your support network know about your journey toward balance.
- **Express Needs:**
    - Be clear about how they can support you.
- **Listen Actively:**
    - Encourage them to share their own experiences and challenges.

Step 3: Engage in Shared Activities
- **Plan Joint Activities:**
    - Participate in hobbies, attend events, or work on projects together.
- **Promote Mutual Growth:**
    - Attend workshops or seminars that interest both of you.

Step 4: Seek Out New Connections
- **Expand Your Network:**
    - Join professional associations, interest groups, or community organizations.
- **Attend Networking Events:**
    - Look for opportunities to meet like-minded individuals.

- **Be Open-Minded:**
  - Embrace diversity in backgrounds and perspectives.

Step 5: Nurture Relationships
- **Show Appreciation:**
  - Acknowledge the support and value others bring to your life.
- **Offer Support:**
  - Be available to assist them in their own goals and challenges.
- **Maintain Boundaries:**
  - Respect each other's time and commitments to ensure a healthy balance.

Closing Thoughts

"Surround yourself with only people who are going to lift you higher."
— *Oprah Winfrey*

Cultivating a support system is more than just building a network; it's about fostering genuine relationships that enrich your life and contribute to your overall well-being. By investing time and effort into connecting with others, you create a foundation of support that can help you navigate the complexities of balancing professional aspirations with personal fulfillment.

Remember that relationships are dynamic and require ongoing attention and care. Be intentional in your interactions, and don't be afraid to seek out new connections that align with your values and goals. As you strengthen your support system, you'll find that not only does your capacity to maintain balance increase, but your life becomes more vibrant and fulfilling.

Next Steps:
- **Complete the Relationship Audit Exercise.**
- **Implement Your Action Plan:**
  - Schedule check-ins and take proactive steps to strengthen your support system.

- **Reflect on the Impact:**
    - Observe how nurturing relationships enhances your work-life balance.

In the final chapter, we'll focus on **Sustaining Balance and Moving Forward**, integrating all the concepts we've explored and creating a personalized roadmap for long-term success and fulfillment.

Side note - A Lesson from the Vietnamese Fisherman

"It is not the man who has too little, but the man who craves more, that is poor." — *Seneca*

During my travels in Vietnam, I found myself in a quaint fishing village along the Mekong Delta. One afternoon, as the sun began its descent, casting hues across the water, I met Hien, a local fisherman. He was returning from his day's work, his boat laden with a modest catch. Intrigued by the serene expression on his face, I struck up a conversation with him.

Hien invited me to his home—a simple wooden house on stilts overlooking the river. There, I met his wife and two children. Their home was humble, with few possessions, but it radiated warmth and contentment. We shared a meal of freshly caught fish, rice, and vegetables from their garden. As we ate, laughter filled the air, and I was enveloped by a profound sense of peace.

Curious about his daily life, I asked Hien about his routine. He explained that he fished in the mornings, spent afternoons with his family, and in the evenings, he played music with his friends. I couldn't help but marvel at the simplicity and balance of his life.

I told him about the hectic pace of my own life, the endless striving for more, and asked if he had ever considered expanding his fishing business. He smiled gently and said, "Why would I? I have enough to feed my family, time to watch my children grow, and moments to enjoy the sunset. What more could I want?"

That evening, as I lay in my guest room listening to the sounds of the river, I reflected on Hien's words. His contentment didn't come from material wealth or professional accolades but from appreciating what he had and living in harmony with his surroundings. It was a powerful reminder that balance isn't about adding more to our lives but finding satisfaction in the simplicity of being.

This encounter left an indelible mark on me. It challenged my perceptions of success and inspired me to reevaluate my own pursuit of balance. Tran's way of life exemplified that sustaining balance is an ongoing process of aligning with our true values and embracing the present moment.

Chapter 8: Sustaining Balance and Moving Forward

"Life is a balance of holding on and letting go." — *Rumi*

As we reach the culmination of our journey together, it's important to recognize that achieving work-life balance isn't a destination but a continuous process. Just as the river flows endlessly, so too does life bring new experiences, challenges, and changes. The key to sustaining balance lies in our ability to adapt, grow, and remain aligned with our core values.

In this final chapter, we'll explore how to create systems that support long-term success, including regular self-check-ins and flexibility in our routines. We'll discuss embracing growth and adapting to life's inevitable changes without losing the equilibrium we've worked so hard to establish. By integrating the insights and practices from previous chapters, you'll be equipped to move forward with confidence and resilience.

Balance Is an Ongoing Process

1. Embracing the Journey

- **Continuous Evolution:** Understand that your needs, priorities, and circumstances will change over time.
- **Mindful Awareness:** Stay present and attentive to how you feel and what you need at different stages of life.
- **Acceptance:** Acknowledge that perfection is neither attainable nor necessary; balance is about making conscious choices moment by moment.

2. The Nature of Balance

- **Dynamic Equilibrium:** Like riding a bicycle, maintaining balance requires constant adjustments.
- **Holistic Integration:** Consider all aspects of your well-being—physical, mental, emotional, and spiritual.
- **Resilience Building:** Develop the capacity to bounce back from setbacks and adapt to new situations.

3. Learning from the Fisherman's Wisdom

- **Simplicity:** Find joy in the simple things and appreciate what you have.
- **Contentment:** Recognize that fulfillment often comes from meaningful relationships and experiences rather than material success.
- **Alignment with Values:** Live in accordance with your core beliefs, as Tran did, to foster lasting satisfaction.

Creating Systems for Long-Term Success

1. Regular Self-Check-Ins

- **Scheduled Reflections:** Set aside time weekly or monthly to assess your well-being and balance.
- **Guided Journaling:** Use prompts to explore your feelings, achievements, and areas needing attention.
- **Mindfulness Practices:** Incorporate meditation or quiet contemplation to tune into your inner state.

2. Flexibility in Routines

- **Adaptable Plans:** Design routines that provide structure but allow for adjustments as needed.
- **Prioritize Self-Care:** Ensure that your schedule includes time for rest, hobbies, and relationships.
- **Balance Structure and Spontaneity:** Leave room for unexpected opportunities and leisure.

3. Goal Setting and Review

- **Short-Term Goals:** Set achievable objectives that align with your values and current priorities.
- **Long-Term Vision:** Keep sight of your overarching aspirations while remaining open to change.
- **Regular Reviews:** Revisit your goals periodically to track progress and make necessary adjustments.

4. Utilizing Support Systems

- **Accountability Partners:** Engage with mentors, friends, or family members who support your journey.

- **Community Engagement:** Participate in groups or networks that encourage balanced living.
- **Professional Guidance:** Seek coaching or counseling if you need additional support.

Embracing Growth and Adapting to Change

1. Cultivating a Growth Mindset

- **Embrace Challenges:** View obstacles as opportunities for learning and development.
- **Continuous Learning:** Stay curious and seek new knowledge and experiences.
- **Self-Compassion:** Be gentle with yourself during times of change or when things don't go as planned.

2. Navigating Life Transitions

- **Anticipate Change:** Recognize that shifts in career, relationships, or personal circumstances are natural.
- **Stay Grounded:** Rely on your core values and support system to navigate transitions.
- **Flexibility:** Be willing to adjust your approach to balance as your life evolves.

3. Letting Go of What's Not Serving You

- **Release Attachments:** Identify habits, beliefs, or commitments that no longer align with your goals.
- **Simplify:** Focus on what truly matters, reducing unnecessary complexities.
- **Embrace the Present:** Practice gratitude and mindfulness to fully experience each moment.

Checklist: Reflecting on Shifts in Priorities

Use the following questions to assess how your priorities may have changed and how you've adapted:

1. **Awareness of Change:**
   - Have you noticed shifts in what's important to you over the past months or years?

- What factors have influenced these changes (e.g., personal growth, life events, new relationships)?

2. **Adapting Your Approach:**
   - How have you adjusted your routines or habits to align with your new priorities?
   - Have you communicated these changes to those affected (e.g., family, colleagues)?

3. **Maintaining Balance:**
   - Are you still honoring your core values in your daily life?
   - What strategies have you employed to sustain balance amid these changes?

4. **Future Considerations:**
   - What upcoming life events or goals might require further adjustments?
   - How can you proactively prepare for these transitions?

Exercise: Reflecting on Your Journey

Objective: Gain insight into how your perspective on work-life balance has evolved since beginning this book.

Instructions:

1. **Set Aside Quiet Time**
   - Find a comfortable space free from distractions.
   - Allow yourself at least 30 minutes for reflection.

2. **Consider the Following Prompts**
   - **Initial Perspective:**
     - What were your beliefs about work-life balance before reading this book?
     - Did you face specific challenges or frustrations?
   - **Key Learnings:**
     - Which chapters or concepts resonated most with you?

- What new insights have you gained about balance?
- **Personal Growth:**
  - How have your thoughts, attitudes, or behaviors changed?
  - Have you implemented any new practices or habits?
- **Impact on Well-Being:**
  - What differences do you notice in your stress levels, relationships, or satisfaction?

3. **Document Your Reflections**
   - Write freely without worrying about structure or grammar.
   - Be honest and compassionate with yourself.

4. **Identify Actionable Insights**
   - Highlight any revelations that can inform your future approach to balance.
   - Consider areas where you wish to continue growing.

Action Plan: Creating Your Long-Term Vision

Objective: Develop a roadmap for maintaining work-life balance over the next six months, incorporating regular self-check-ins and adjustments to your routine.

Steps:

1. **Define Your Vision**
   - **Envision Your Balanced Life:**
     - Describe what an ideal work-life balance looks like for you.
     - Consider all aspects of your life—career, relationships, health, personal growth.
   - **Set Clear Goals:**
     - Identify specific, measurable objectives

that align with your vision.

- Examples: "Exercise three times a week," "Limit work emails after 7 PM," "Spend quality time with family on weekends."

2. Develop a Flexible Plan

- **Create a Timeline:**
  - Outline milestones or checkpoints over the next six months.
  - Allow for adjustments as needed.

- **Establish Routines:**
  - Design daily or weekly schedules that support your goals.
  - Incorporate time for self-care, hobbies, and relaxation.

3. Implement Regular Self-Check-Ins

- **Schedule Reflection Times:**
  - Set reminders for weekly or monthly reviews.
  - Use these sessions to assess progress and well-being.

- **Use Reflection Tools:**
  - Maintain a journal, use apps, or create checklists to guide your evaluations.

4. Adapt and Evolve

- **Stay Open to Change:**
  - Be prepared to modify your plan in response to new circumstances.
  - Embrace flexibility while staying true to your core values.

- **Seek Feedback:**
  - Engage with your support system for insights and encouragement.
  - Consider professional guidance if needed.

5. Celebrate Successes

- **Acknowledge Achievements:**

- Recognize and reward yourself for milestones reached.
- Reflect on the positive impact of your efforts.

Closing Thoughts

"The secret of change is to focus all of your energy not on fighting the old, but on building the new." — Socrates

As we conclude this journey, remember that sustaining balance is a lifelong endeavor. It's about making intentional choices each day that align with your authentic self. Like the fisherman in Vietnam, find contentment in the simplicity of living according to your values.

Life will inevitably bring changes—some expected, others unforeseen. By cultivating adaptability, nurturing your support systems, and staying connected to your inner compass, you can navigate these shifts with grace and resilience.

Thank you for allowing me to be a part of your quest for balance. I hope the insights, exercises, and reflections within this book serve as a valuable resource as you move forward. May you continue to grow, adapt, and thrive, embracing each moment with mindfulness and joy.

Next Steps

- **Implement Your Long-Term Vision:**
  - Begin taking actionable steps toward your goals.
- **Maintain Regular Self-Check-Ins:**
  - Stay attuned to your needs and make adjustments as necessary.
- **Stay Connected:**
  - Continue cultivating relationships that support your balanced lifestyle.
- **Embrace the Journey:**
  - Remember that balance is an ongoing process— be patient and kind to yourself.

Final Reflection:

"Your life is a story of transition. You are always leaving one chapter behind while moving on to the next." — Anonymous

As you turn the page to the next chapter of your life, carry with you the wisdom gained and the commitment to living a balanced, fulfilling existence. The path ahead is yours to shape—walk it with intention, courage, and an open heart.

Conclusion: A Balanced Life is a Fulfilled Life

Recap of Our Journey Together

"The joy of life is not in the grand gestures, but in the simple moments where we find harmony within ourselves and the world around us."

As we conclude this exploration of achieving work-life balance, let's reflect on the key lessons we've uncovered along the way:

- **Understanding the Imbalance:** We began by recognizing the signs of imbalance in our lives, acknowledging the toll it takes on our health, relationships, and overall well-being. We challenged the notion of hustle culture and redefined success on our own terms.

- **Defining Your Core Values:** We delved deep into self-discovery, identifying what truly matters to us. By aligning our actions with our core values, we laid the foundation for a more authentic and fulfilling life.

- **The Power of Time Management:** We explored practical tools and techniques to manage our most precious resource—time. By prioritizing effectively and breaking down overwhelming tasks, we regained control over our schedules.

- **Setting Boundaries for Success:** We learned the

importance of saying "no" and setting healthy boundaries to protect our personal time and energy. Clear communication with others became a key strategy in maintaining balance.

- **Building Healthy Habits for the Long Term:** We recognized that our daily habits significantly impact our ability to sustain balance. By adopting a holistic approach and integrating positive routines, we supported our overall well-being.

- **Managing Stress and Avoiding Burnout:** We identified signs of stress and burnout, embracing techniques such as mindfulness and breathing exercises to navigate challenges without losing equilibrium.

- **Cultivating a Support System:** We acknowledged the vital role relationships play in our journey, fostering meaningful connections that uplift and support us.

- **Sustaining Balance and Moving Forward:** We understood that balance is an ongoing process, requiring adaptability and self-awareness. By creating systems for long-term success, we prepared ourselves to embrace growth and life's inevitable changes.

Throughout this journey, we've emphasized that balance is not a static goal but a dynamic practice. It involves continuous self-reflection, adjustment, and compassion toward ourselves.

A Final Message of Encouragement

Dear Reader,

Balance is indeed achievable, but it is a practice, not perfection. There will be days when the scales tip, and that's okay. What's important is your commitment to return to center, to listen to your inner voice, and to honor your needs.

Remember to be patient with yourself. Celebrate small victories and learn from setbacks without harsh judgment. Persistence is key—each step you take, no matter how small, contributes to the larger journey of living a balanced and fulfilling life.

You possess the strength, wisdom, and resilience to craft the life you envision. Trust in your abilities, embrace the process, and know that you are not alone on this path.

Acknowledgment

Writing this book has been a trans-formative experience, and it would not have been possible without the support and inspiration of many remarkable individuals.

To my beloved wife, thank you for being my anchor and constant source of love. Your unwavering support, understanding, and encouragement have been the bedrock upon which this work was built. You are my partner in every adventure, and I am eternally grateful for your presence in my life.

To my family and friends, your belief in me fueled my motivation. The laughter, conversations, and shared moments have enriched my life beyond measure.

I extend my deepest gratitude to the countless souls we encountered during our travels—the monks in India who imparted timeless wisdom, the shamans in Thailand who opened doors to new perspectives, the locals in Australia and Malaysia who welcomed us with open hearts, and the professionals in Japan who shared their insights on harmony and discipline. Each of you has contributed a unique thread to the tapestry of this book.

Your stories, teachings, and kindness have not only informed these pages but have also profoundly impacted my personal journey toward balance. Thank you for sharing your cultures, traditions, and philosophies. Your influence is woven throughout this work.

A Note to the Reader

This book reflects my personal experiences and perspectives gathered over years of exploration and introspection. While I hope the insights and strategies shared herein resonate with you, please remember that everyone's journey is unique.

If you find yourself struggling or in need of additional support, I encourage you to seek guidance from professionals, such as counselors, coaches, or medical practitioners. They can provide personalized assistance tailored to your specific circumstances.

In Gratitude and Solidarity

Thank you, dear reader, for embarking on this journey with me. Your willingness to engage with these ideas and apply them to your life is both courageous and inspiring.

As you move forward, carry with you the knowledge that balance is within your reach. Embrace each day with mindfulness, compassion, and a steadfast commitment to your well-being.

Wishing you harmony, fulfillment, and endless moments of joy.

With heartfelt appreciation.

please leve an honest review and send to my private email your comments

secondchapter222@gmail.com

www.ingramcontent.com/pod-product-compliance
Lightning Source LLC
Chambersburg PA
CBHW070119230526
45472CB00004B/1334